THIS JOURNAL BELONGS TO

# THE
# HIKER'S JOURNAL

## HOW TO USE THIS BOOK

WELCOME TO YOUR JOURNAL, a place to look back on the long days you've spent on the trail, write down reminders and ideas for the future, and keep track of your most memorable hiking experiences.

This journal is divided into three parts. The first, Hiking Logs, is the heart of the book. Here, you can write down the details about every trail you hike, allowing you to keep track of your favorites and everything you saw and experienced on each excursion. Each log has a page with spaces for key information about the trail, the weather, and everything you saw on your hike, plus a lined page you can use for additional notes. At the beginning of the section, you'll find a DIY index where you can enter the location and date for each log entry as you work through the journal.

Following the hiking logs, there is a section with blank pages where you can include any extra notes and sketches—map your favorite hikes, keep running equipment lists, or just reminisce about a great day outdoors. The final section, Hiking Checklists, gives you a place to list your favorite trips, hiking bucket list, the gear you think is essential, the mountains you've climbed, and all the animals you've seen (so far).

### HAPPY HIKING!

# HIKING LOGS

# HIKING LOG INDEX

| LOG # | LOCATION | DATE |
|-------|----------|------|
|       |          |      |
|       |          |      |
|       |          |      |
|       |          |      |
|       |          |      |
|       |          |      |
|       |          |      |
|       |          |      |
|       |          |      |
|       |          |      |
|       |          |      |
|       |          |      |
|       |          |      |
|       |          |      |
|       |          |      |
|       |          |      |
|       |          |      |
|       |          |      |

| LOG # | LOCATION | DATE |
|-------|----------|------|
|       |          |      |
|       |          |      |
|       |          |      |
|       |          |      |
|       |          |      |
|       |          |      |
|       |          |      |
|       |          |      |
|       |          |      |
|       |          |      |
|       |          |      |
|       |          |      |
|       |          |      |
|       |          |      |
|       |          |      |
|       |          |      |
|       |          |      |

# HIKING LOG INDEX

| LOG # | LOCATION | DATE |
|---|---|---|
|  |  |  |
|  |  |  |
|  |  |  |
|  |  |  |
|  |  |  |
|  |  |  |
|  |  |  |
|  |  |  |
|  |  |  |
|  |  |  |
|  |  |  |
|  |  |  |
|  |  |  |
|  |  |  |
|  |  |  |
|  |  |  |
|  |  |  |
|  |  |  |

| LOG # | LOCATION | DATE |
|-------|----------|------|
|       |          |      |
|       |          |      |
|       |          |      |
|       |          |      |
|       |          |      |
|       |          |      |
|       |          |      |
|       |          |      |
|       |          |      |
|       |          |      |
|       |          |      |
|       |          |      |
|       |          |      |
|       |          |      |
|       |          |      |
|       |          |      |
|       |          |      |
|       |          |      |

# HIKING LOG

LOG #

**DATE**

**START TIME**

**END TIME**

**LOCATION**

## OBSERVATIONS

**WEATHER** _____

**ROUTE/TRAIL NAMES** _____

_____

_____

_____

_____

**HIKE TYPE**   loop   out and back   one way   day trip   overnight   other _____

**DISTANCE** _____

**ELEVATION** (gain/loss) _____

**DIFFICULTY**   1   2   3   4   5   6   7   8   9   10

**TERRAIN NOTES** _____

_____

**FACILITIES/WATER** _____

**WILDLIFE OBSERVED** _____

_____

_____

**HIGHLIGHTS** _____

_____

_____

OVERALL RATING

# HIKING LOG

LOG #

**DATE**

**START TIME**

**END TIME**

**LOCATION**

**OBSERVATIONS**

**WEATHER** _____

**ROUTE/TRAIL NAMES** _____

_____

_____

_____

_____

**HIKE TYPE**
loop    out and back    one way    day trip    overnight    other _____

**DISTANCE** _____

**ELEVATION** (gain/loss) _____

**DIFFICULTY**    1    2    3    4    5    6    7    8    9    10

**TERRAIN NOTES** _____

_____

**FACILITIES/WATER** _____

**WILDLIFE OBSERVED** _____

_____

_____

**HIGHLIGHTS** _____

_____

_____

_____

**OVERALL RATING**

# HIKING LOG

LOG #

DATE

START TIME

END TIME

LOCATION

OBSERVATIONS

**WEATHER** _____

**ROUTE/TRAIL NAMES** _____

_____

_____

_____

_____

**HIKE TYPE**   loop   out and back   one way   day trip   overnight   other _____

**DISTANCE** _____

**ELEVATION** (gain/loss) _____

| **DIFFICULTY** | 1 | 2 | 3 | 4 | 5 | 6 | 7 | 8 | 9 | 10 |
|---|---|---|---|---|---|---|---|---|---|---|

**TERRAIN NOTES** _____

_____

**FACILITIES/WATER** _____

**WILDLIFE OBSERVED** _____

_____

_____

**HIGHLIGHTS** _____

_____

_____

_____

**OVERALL RATING**

# HIKING LOG

**LOG #**

**DATE**

**START TIME**

**END TIME**

**LOCATION**

**OBSERVATIONS**

WEATHER _____

ROUTE/TRAIL NAMES _____

_____

_____

_____

_____

HIKE TYPE

loop    out and back    one way    day trip    overnight    other _____

DISTANCE _____

ELEVATION (gain/loss) _____

| DIFFICULTY | 1 | 2 | 3 | 4 | 5 | 6 | 7 | 8 | 9 | 10 |
|---|---|---|---|---|---|---|---|---|---|---|

TERRAIN NOTES _____

_____

FACILITIES/WATER _____

WILDLIFE OBSERVED _____

_____

HIGHLIGHTS _____

_____

_____

_____

OVERALL RATING

# HIKING LOG

LOG #

DATE

START TIME

END TIME

LOCATION

OBSERVATIONS

**WEATHER** _____

**ROUTE/TRAIL NAMES** _____

_____

_____

_____

_____

**HIKE TYPE**    loop    out and back    one way    day trip    overnight    other _____

**DISTANCE** _____

**ELEVATION** (gain/loss) _____

| DIFFICULTY | 1 | 2 | 3 | 4 | 5 | 6 | 7 | 8 | 9 | 10 |
|---|---|---|---|---|---|---|---|---|---|---|

**TERRAIN NOTES** _____

_____

**FACILITIES/WATER** _____

**WILDLIFE OBSERVED** _____

_____

_____

**HIGHLIGHTS** _____

_____

_____

_____

OVERALL RATING

# HIKING LOG

LOG #

**DATE**

**START TIME**

**END TIME**

**LOCATION**

**OBSERVATIONS**

WEATHER _____

ROUTE/TRAIL NAMES _____

_____

_____

_____

_____

HIKE TYPE    loop    out and back    one way    day trip    overnight    other _____

DISTANCE _____

ELEVATION (gain/loss) _____

| DIFFICULTY | 1 | 2 | 3 | 4 | 5 | 6 | 7 | 8 | 9 | 10 |
|---|---|---|---|---|---|---|---|---|---|---|

TERRAIN NOTES _____

_____

FACILITIES/WATER _____

WILDLIFE OBSERVED _____

_____

HIGHLIGHTS _____

_____

_____

_____

OVERALL RATING

# HIKING LOG

LOG #

DATE

START TIME

END TIME

LOCATION

## OBSERVATIONS

WEATHER _____

ROUTE/TRAIL NAMES _____

_____

_____

_____

_____

HIKE TYPE    ○ loop    ⇄ out and back    → one way    ☀ day trip    ⛺ overnight    other _____

DISTANCE _____

ELEVATION (gain/loss) _____

| DIFFICULTY | 1 | 2 | 3 | 4 | 5 | 6 | 7 | 8 | 9 | 10 |

TERRAIN NOTES _____

_____

FACILITIES/WATER _____

WILDLIFE OBSERVED _____

_____

HIGHLIGHTS _____

_____

_____

_____

OVERALL RATING

# HIKING LOG

LOG #

**DATE**

**START TIME**

**END TIME**

**LOCATION**

**OBSERVATIONS**

**WEATHER** _____

**ROUTE/TRAIL NAMES** _____

_____

_____

_____

_____

**HIKE TYPE**   loop   out and back   one way   day trip   overnight   other _____

**DISTANCE** _____

**ELEVATION** (gain/loss) _____

**DIFFICULTY**   1   2   3   4   5   6   7   8   9   10

**TERRAIN NOTES** _____

_____

**FACILITIES/WATER** _____

**WILDLIFE OBSERVED** _____

_____

_____

**HIGHLIGHTS** _____

_____

_____

_____

**OVERALL RATING**

# HIKING LOG

LOG #

**DATE**

**START TIME**

**END TIME**

**LOCATION**

**OBSERVATIONS**

WEATHER _____

ROUTE/TRAIL NAMES _____

_____

_____

_____

_____

HIKE TYPE    loop    out and back    one way    day trip    overnight    other _____

DISTANCE _____

ELEVATION (gain/loss) _____

| DIFFICULTY | 1 | 2 | 3 | 4 | 5 | 6 | 7 | 8 | 9 | 10 |
|---|---|---|---|---|---|---|---|---|---|---|

TERRAIN NOTES _____

_____

FACILITIES/WATER _____

WILDLIFE OBSERVED _____

_____

HIGHLIGHTS _____

_____

_____

_____

OVERALL RATING 🥾 🥾 🥾 🥾 🥾

# HIKING LOG

LOG #

**DATE**

**START TIME**

**END TIME**

**LOCATION**

**OBSERVATIONS**

WEATHER _____

ROUTE/TRAIL NAMES _____

_____

_____

_____

_____

HIKE TYPE    loop    out and back    one way    day trip    overnight    other _____

DISTANCE _____

ELEVATION (gain/loss) _____

| DIFFICULTY | 1 | 2 | 3 | 4 | 5 | 6 | 7 | 8 | 9 | 10 |
|---|---|---|---|---|---|---|---|---|---|---|

TERRAIN NOTES _____

_____

FACILITIES/WATER _____

WILDLIFE OBSERVED _____

_____

HIGHLIGHTS _____

_____

_____

_____

OVERALL RATING

# HIKING LOG

LOG #

**DATE**

**START TIME**

**END TIME**

**LOCATION**

**OBSERVATIONS**

WEATHER _____

ROUTE/TRAIL NAMES _____

_____

_____

_____

_____

HIKE TYPE

loop     out and back     one way     day trip     overnight     other _____

DISTANCE _____

ELEVATION (gain/loss) _____

| DIFFICULTY | 1 | 2 | 3 | 4 | 5 | 6 | 7 | 8 | 9 | 10 |
|---|---|---|---|---|---|---|---|---|---|---|

TERRAIN NOTES _____

_____

FACILITIES/WATER _____

WILDLIFE OBSERVED _____

_____

HIGHLIGHTS _____

_____

_____

_____

OVERALL RATING

# HIKING LOG

LOG #

**DATE**

**START TIME**

**END TIME**

**LOCATION**

**OBSERVATIONS**

WEATHER _____

ROUTE/TRAIL NAMES _____

_____

_____

_____

_____

HIKE TYPE   ◯ loop   ⇄ out and back   → one way   ☀ day trip   ⛺ overnight   other _____

DISTANCE _____

ELEVATION (gain/loss) _____

| DIFFICULTY | 1 | 2 | 3 | 4 | 5 | 6 | 7 | 8 | 9 | 10 |
|---|---|---|---|---|---|---|---|---|---|---|

TERRAIN NOTES _____

_____

FACILITIES/WATER _____

WILDLIFE OBSERVED _____

_____

_____

HIGHLIGHTS _____

_____

_____

_____

OVERALL RATING  👢 👢 👢 👢 👢

# HIKING LOG

LOG #

**DATE**

**START TIME**

**END TIME**

**LOCATION**

**OBSERVATIONS**

**WEATHER** _____

**ROUTE/TRAIL NAMES** _____

_____

_____

_____

_____

**HIKE TYPE**  loop   out and back   one way   day trip   overnight   other _____

**DISTANCE** _____

**ELEVATION** (gain/loss) _____

| DIFFICULTY | 1 | 2 | 3 | 4 | 5 | 6 | 7 | 8 | 9 | 10 |
|---|---|---|---|---|---|---|---|---|---|---|

**TERRAIN NOTES** _____

_____

**FACILITIES/WATER** _____

**WILDLIFE OBSERVED** _____

_____

_____

**HIGHLIGHTS** _____

_____

_____

_____

OVERALL RATING

# HIKING LOG

LOG #

**DATE**

**START TIME**

**END TIME**

**LOCATION**

**OBSERVATIONS**

WEATHER _____

ROUTE/TRAIL NAMES _____

_____

_____

_____

_____

HIKE TYPE

loop    out and back    one way    day trip    overnight    other _____

DISTANCE _____

ELEVATION (gain/loss) _____

| DIFFICULTY | 1 | 2 | 3 | 4 | 5 | 6 | 7 | 8 | 9 | 10 |
|---|---|---|---|---|---|---|---|---|---|---|

TERRAIN NOTES _____

_____

FACILITIES/WATER _____

WILDLIFE OBSERVED _____

_____

HIGHLIGHTS _____

_____

_____

_____

OVERALL RATING

# HIKING LOG

LOG #

DATE

START TIME

END TIME

LOCATION

OBSERVATIONS

WEATHER _____

ROUTE/TRAIL NAMES _____
_____
_____
_____
_____

HIKE TYPE   ⟲        ⇄            →         ☀         ⛺        other _____
          loop   out and back   one way   day trip   overnight

DISTANCE _____

ELEVATION (gain/loss) _____

| DIFFICULTY | 1 | 2 | 3 | 4 | 5 | 6 | 7 | 8 | 9 | 10 |
|---|---|---|---|---|---|---|---|---|---|---|

TERRAIN NOTES _____
_____

FACILITIES/WATER _____

WILDLIFE OBSERVED _____
_____
_____

HIGHLIGHTS _____
_____
_____
_____

OVERALL RATING  🥾 🥾 🥾 🥾 🥾

# HIKING LOG

LOG #

DATE

START TIME

END TIME

LOCATION

OBSERVATIONS

WEATHER _____

ROUTE/TRAIL NAMES _____

_____

_____

_____

_____

HIKE TYPE    loop    out and back    one way    day trip    overnight    other _____

DISTANCE _____

ELEVATION (gain/loss) _____

## DIFFICULTY    1   2   3   4   5   6   7   8   9   10

TERRAIN NOTES _____

_____

FACILITIES/WATER _____

WILDLIFE OBSERVED _____

_____

_____

HIGHLIGHTS _____

_____

_____

_____

OVERALL RATING

# HIKING LOG

**LOG #**

**DATE**

**START TIME**

**END TIME**

**LOCATION**

**OBSERVATIONS**

WEATHER _____

ROUTE/TRAIL NAMES _____

_____

_____

_____

_____

HIKE TYPE  ⟲ loop   ⇄ out and back   → one way   ☀ day trip   ⛺ overnight   other _____

DISTANCE _____

ELEVATION (gain/loss) _____

| DIFFICULTY | 1 | 2 | 3 | 4 | 5 | 6 | 7 | 8 | 9 | 10 |
|---|---|---|---|---|---|---|---|---|---|---|

TERRAIN NOTES _____

_____

FACILITIES/WATER _____

WILDLIFE OBSERVED _____

_____

_____

HIGHLIGHTS _____

_____

_____

_____

OVERALL RATING  👢 👢 👢 👢 👢

# HIKING LOG

LOG #

**DATE**

**START TIME**

**END TIME**

**LOCATION**

**OBSERVATIONS**

WEATHER _____

ROUTE/TRAIL NAMES _____

_____

_____

_____

_____

HIKE TYPE    loop    out and back    one way    day trip    overnight    other _____

DISTANCE _____

ELEVATION (gain/loss) _____

**DIFFICULTY**    1    2    3    4    5    6    7    8    9    10

TERRAIN NOTES _____

_____

FACILITIES/WATER _____

WILDLIFE OBSERVED _____

_____

_____

HIGHLIGHTS _____

_____

_____

OVERALL RATING

# HIKING LOG

LOG #

**DATE**

**START TIME**

**END TIME**

**LOCATION**

**OBSERVATIONS**

**WEATHER** _____

**ROUTE/TRAIL NAMES** _____

_____

_____

_____

_____

**HIKE TYPE**    ↻ loop    ⇄ out and back    → one way    ☀ day trip    ⛺ overnight    other _____

**DISTANCE** _____

**ELEVATION** (gain/loss) _____

**DIFFICULTY**    1    2    3    4    5    6    7    8    9    10

**TERRAIN NOTES** _____

_____

**FACILITIES/WATER** _____

**WILDLIFE OBSERVED** _____

_____

_____

**HIGHLIGHTS** _____

_____

_____

_____

**OVERALL RATING**    👢  👢  👢  👢  👢

# HIKING LOG

LOG #

**DATE**

**START TIME**

**END TIME**

**LOCATION**

OBSERVATIONS

WEATHER _____

ROUTE/TRAIL NAMES _____

_____

_____

_____

_____

HIKE TYPE    loop    out and back    one way    day trip    overnight    other _____

DISTANCE _____

ELEVATION (gain/loss) _____

| DIFFICULTY | 1 | 2 | 3 | 4 | 5 | 6 | 7 | 8 | 9 | 10 |
|---|---|---|---|---|---|---|---|---|---|---|

TERRAIN NOTES _____

_____

FACILITIES/WATER _____

WILDLIFE OBSERVED _____

_____

_____

HIGHLIGHTS _____

_____

_____

_____

OVERALL RATING

# HIKING LOG

LOG #

**DATE**

**START TIME**

**END TIME**

**LOCATION**

**OBSERVATIONS**

WEATHER _____

ROUTE/TRAIL NAMES _____

_____

_____

_____

_____

HIKE TYPE   loop   out and back   one way   day trip   overnight   other _____

DISTANCE _____

ELEVATION (gain/loss) _____

**DIFFICULTY**    1    2    3    4    5    6    7    8    9    10

TERRAIN NOTES _____

_____

FACILITIES/WATER _____

WILDLIFE OBSERVED _____

_____

_____

HIGHLIGHTS _____

_____

_____

_____

OVERALL RATING

# HIKING LOG

LOG #

**DATE**

**START TIME**

**END TIME**

**LOCATION**

**OBSERVATIONS**

**WEATHER** _____

**ROUTE/TRAIL NAMES** _____

_____

_____

_____

_____

**HIKE TYPE**   loop   out and back   one way   day trip   overnight   other _____

**DISTANCE** _____

**ELEVATION** (gain/loss) _____

| DIFFICULTY | 1 | 2 | 3 | 4 | 5 | 6 | 7 | 8 | 9 | 10 |
|---|---|---|---|---|---|---|---|---|---|---|

**TERRAIN NOTES** _____

_____

**FACILITIES/WATER** _____

**WILDLIFE OBSERVED** _____

_____

_____

**HIGHLIGHTS** _____

_____

_____

_____

**OVERALL RATING**

# HIKING LOG

LOG #

**DATE**

**START TIME**

**END TIME**

**LOCATION**

**OBSERVATIONS**

WEATHER _____

ROUTE/TRAIL NAMES _____

_____

_____

_____

_____

HIKE TYPE    loop    out and back    one way    day trip    overnight    other _____

DISTANCE _____

ELEVATION (gain/loss) _____

| DIFFICULTY | 1 | 2 | 3 | 4 | 5 | 6 | 7 | 8 | 9 | 10 |

TERRAIN NOTES _____

_____

FACILITIES/WATER _____

WILDLIFE OBSERVED _____

_____

_____

HIGHLIGHTS _____

_____

_____

_____

OVERALL RATING

# HIKING LOG

LOG #

**DATE**

**START TIME**

**END TIME**

**LOCATION**

**OBSERVATIONS**

**WEATHER** _____

**ROUTE/TRAIL NAMES** _____
_____
_____
_____
_____

**HIKE TYPE**　　loop　　out and back　　one way　　day trip　　overnight　　other _____

**DISTANCE** _____

**ELEVATION** (gain/loss) _____

**DIFFICULTY**　　1　　2　　3　　4　　5　　6　　7　　8　　9　　10

**TERRAIN NOTES** _____
_____

**FACILITIES/WATER** _____

**WILDLIFE OBSERVED** _____
_____
_____

**HIGHLIGHTS** _____
_____
_____
_____

**OVERALL RATING**

# HIKING LOG

LOG #

**DATE**

**START TIME**

**END TIME**

**LOCATION**

**OBSERVATIONS**

WEATHER _____

ROUTE/TRAIL NAMES _____

_____

_____

_____

_____

HIKE TYPE   loop   out and back   one way   day trip   overnight   other _____

DISTANCE _____

ELEVATION (gain/loss) _____

DIFFICULTY    1    2    3    4    5    6    7    8    9    10

TERRAIN NOTES _____

_____

FACILITIES/WATER _____

WILDLIFE OBSERVED _____

_____

_____

HIGHLIGHTS _____

_____

_____

_____

OVERALL RATING

# HIKING LOG

LOG #

**DATE**

**START TIME**

**END TIME**

**LOCATION**

**OBSERVATIONS**

WEATHER _____

ROUTE/TRAIL NAMES _____
_____
_____
_____
_____

HIKE TYPE  ⟳ loop   ⇄ out and back   → one way   ☀ day trip   ⛺ overnight   other _____

DISTANCE _____

ELEVATION (gain/loss) _____

## DIFFICULTY   1   2   3   4   5   6   7   8   9   10

TERRAIN NOTES _____
_____

FACILITIES/WATER _____

WILDLIFE OBSERVED _____
_____
_____

HIGHLIGHTS _____
_____
_____
_____

OVERALL RATING

# HIKING LOG

LOG #

DATE

START TIME

END TIME

LOCATION

OBSERVATIONS

**WEATHER** _____

**ROUTE/TRAIL NAMES** _____

_____

_____

_____

_____

**HIKE TYPE**    ↻ loop    ⇄ out and back    → one way    ☀ day trip    ⛺ overnight    other _____

**DISTANCE** _____

**ELEVATION** (gain/loss) _____

**DIFFICULTY**    1    2    3    4    5    6    7    8    9    10

**TERRAIN NOTES** _____

_____

**FACILITIES/WATER** _____

**WILDLIFE OBSERVED** _____

_____

_____

**HIGHLIGHTS** _____

_____

_____

**OVERALL RATING**    👢 👢 👢 👢 👢

# HIKING LOG

LOG #

**DATE**

**START TIME**

**END TIME**

**LOCATION**

**OBSERVATIONS**

WEATHER _____

ROUTE/TRAIL NAMES _____

_____

_____

_____

_____

HIKE TYPE   ○ loop   ⇄ out and back   → one way   ☀ day trip   ⛺ overnight   other _____

DISTANCE _____

ELEVATION (gain/loss) _____

**DIFFICULTY**   1   2   3   4   5   6   7   8   9   10

TERRAIN NOTES _____

_____

FACILITIES/WATER _____

WILDLIFE OBSERVED _____

_____

_____

HIGHLIGHTS _____

_____

_____

_____

OVERALL RATING   👢 👢 👢 👢 👢

# HIKING LOG

LOG #

**DATE**

**START TIME**

**END TIME**

**LOCATION**

**OBSERVATIONS**

WEATHER _____

ROUTE/TRAIL NAMES _____

_____

_____

_____

_____

HIKE TYPE
loop   out and back   one way   day trip   overnight   other _____

DISTANCE _____

ELEVATION (gain/loss) _____

| DIFFICULTY | 1 | 2 | 3 | 4 | 5 | 6 | 7 | 8 | 9 | 10 |

TERRAIN NOTES _____

_____

FACILITIES/WATER _____

WILDLIFE OBSERVED _____

_____

_____

HIGHLIGHTS _____

_____

_____

_____

OVERALL RATING

# HIKING LOG

LOG #

**DATE**

**START TIME**

**END TIME**

**LOCATION**

**OBSERVATIONS**

WEATHER _____

ROUTE/TRAIL NAMES _____

_____

_____

_____

_____

HIKE TYPE

loop    out and back    one way    day trip    overnight    other _____

DISTANCE _____

ELEVATION (gain/loss) _____

DIFFICULTY    1    2    3    4    5    6    7    8    9    10

TERRAIN NOTES _____

_____

FACILITIES/WATER _____

WILDLIFE OBSERVED _____

_____

_____

HIGHLIGHTS _____

_____

_____

_____

OVERALL RATING

# HIKING LOG

LOG #

| DATE | START TIME | END TIME |
|------|-----------|----------|

LOCATION

## OBSERVATIONS

**WEATHER** _____

**ROUTE/TRAIL NAMES** _____

_____

_____

_____

_____

**HIKE TYPE**    loop    out and back    one way    day trip    overnight    other _____

**DISTANCE** _____

**ELEVATION** (gain/loss) _____

**DIFFICULTY**    1    2    3    4    5    6    7    8    9    10

**TERRAIN NOTES** _____

_____

**FACILITIES/WATER** _____

**WILDLIFE OBSERVED** _____

_____

_____

**HIGHLIGHTS** _____

_____

_____

_____

**OVERALL RATING**

# HIKING LOG

LOG #

DATE

START TIME

END TIME

LOCATION

OBSERVATIONS

WEATHER _____

ROUTE/TRAIL NAMES _____

_____

_____

_____

_____

HIKE TYPE   loop   out and back   one way   day trip   overnight   other _____

DISTANCE _____

ELEVATION (gain/loss) _____

## DIFFICULTY   1   2   3   4   5   6   7   8   9   10

TERRAIN NOTES _____

_____

FACILITIES/WATER _____

WILDLIFE OBSERVED _____

_____

_____

HIGHLIGHTS _____

_____

_____

_____

OVERALL RATING

# HIKING LOG

**LOG #**

**DATE**

**START TIME**

**END TIME**

**LOCATION**

**OBSERVATIONS**

WEATHER _____

ROUTE/TRAIL NAMES _____

_____

_____

_____

_____

HIKE TYPE   loop   out and back   one way   day trip   overnight   other _____

DISTANCE _____

ELEVATION (gain/loss) _____

**DIFFICULTY**   1   2   3   4   5   6   7   8   9   10

TERRAIN NOTES _____

_____

FACILITIES/WATER _____

WILDLIFE OBSERVED _____

_____

HIGHLIGHTS _____

_____

_____

_____

OVERALL RATING

# HIKING LOG

LOG #

**DATE**

**START TIME**

**END TIME**

**LOCATION**

**OBSERVATIONS**

WEATHER _____

ROUTE/TRAIL NAMES _____

_____

_____

_____

_____

HIKE TYPE    ⟳          ⇄            →         ☀         ⛺
           loop    out and back    one way   day trip   overnight    other _____

DISTANCE _____

ELEVATION (gain/loss) _____

DIFFICULTY    1    2    3    4    5    6    7    8    9    10

TERRAIN NOTES _____

_____

FACILITIES/WATER _____

WILDLIFE OBSERVED _____

_____

_____

HIGHLIGHTS _____

_____

_____

_____

OVERALL RATING    🥾  🥾  🥾  🥾  🥾

# HIKING LOG

LOG #

DATE

START TIME

END TIME

LOCATION

OBSERVATIONS

**WEATHER** _____

**ROUTE/TRAIL NAMES** _____
_____
_____
_____
_____

**HIKE TYPE**   ◯ loop   ⇄ out and back   → one way   ☀ day trip   ⛺ overnight   other _____

**DISTANCE** _____

**ELEVATION** (gain/loss) _____

**DIFFICULTY**   1   2   3   4   5   6   7   8   9   10

**TERRAIN NOTES** _____
_____

**FACILITIES/WATER** _____

**WILDLIFE OBSERVED** _____
_____
_____

**HIGHLIGHTS** _____
_____
_____
_____

**OVERALL RATING**   🥾 🥾 🥾 🥾 🥾

# HIKING LOG

**LOG #**

**DATE**

**START TIME**

**END TIME**

**LOCATION**

**OBSERVATIONS**

**WEATHER** _____

**ROUTE/TRAIL NAMES** _____

_____

_____

_____

_____

**HIKE TYPE**    ○ loop    ⇄ out and back    → one way    ☀ day trip    ⛺ overnight    other _____

**DISTANCE** _____

**ELEVATION** (gain/loss) _____

| DIFFICULTY | 1 | 2 | 3 | 4 | 5 | 6 | 7 | 8 | 9 | 10 |
|---|---|---|---|---|---|---|---|---|---|---|

**TERRAIN NOTES** _____

_____

**FACILITIES/WATER** _____

**WILDLIFE OBSERVED** _____

_____

_____

**HIGHLIGHTS** _____

_____

_____

_____

**OVERALL RATING**

# HIKING LOG

LOG #

DATE

START TIME

END TIME

LOCATION

OBSERVATIONS

**WEATHER** _____

**ROUTE/TRAIL NAMES** _____

_____

_____

_____

_____

**HIKE TYPE**  ⟳ loop   ⇄ out and back   → one way   ☀ day trip   ⛺ overnight   other _____

**DISTANCE** _____

**ELEVATION** (gain/loss) _____

**DIFFICULTY**   1   2   3   4   5   6   7   8   9   10

**TERRAIN NOTES** _____

_____

**FACILITIES/WATER** _____

**WILDLIFE OBSERVED** _____

_____

_____

**HIGHLIGHTS** _____

_____

_____

_____

OVERALL RATING

# HIKING LOG

LOG #

**DATE**

**START TIME**

**END TIME**

**LOCATION**

OBSERVATIONS

**WEATHER** _____

**ROUTE/TRAIL NAMES** _____
_____
_____
_____
_____

**HIKE TYPE**   ↻ loop    ⇄ out and back    → one way    ☀ day trip    ⛺ overnight    other _____

**DISTANCE** _____

**ELEVATION** (gain/loss) _____

**DIFFICULTY**    1    2    3    4    5    6    7    8    9    10

**TERRAIN NOTES** _____
_____

**FACILITIES/WATER** _____

**WILDLIFE OBSERVED** _____
_____
_____

**HIGHLIGHTS** _____
_____
_____
_____

**OVERALL RATING**   👢 👢 👢 👢 👢

# HIKING LOG

**LOG #**

**DATE**

**START TIME**

**END TIME**

**LOCATION**

**OBSERVATIONS**

WEATHER _____

ROUTE/TRAIL NAMES _____
_____
_____
_____
_____

HIKE TYPE    ↻ loop    ⇄ out and back    → one way    ☀ day trip    ⛺ overnight    other _____

DISTANCE _____

ELEVATION (gain/loss) _____

| DIFFICULTY | 1 | 2 | 3 | 4 | 5 | 6 | 7 | 8 | 9 | 10 |
|---|---|---|---|---|---|---|---|---|---|---|

TERRAIN NOTES _____
_____

FACILITIES/WATER _____

WILDLIFE OBSERVED _____
_____
_____

HIGHLIGHTS _____
_____
_____
_____

OVERALL RATING  🥾 🥾 🥾 🥾 🥾

# HIKING LOG

LOG #

**DATE**

**START TIME**

**END TIME**

**LOCATION**

**OBSERVATIONS**

**WEATHER** _____

**ROUTE/TRAIL NAMES** _____

_____

_____

_____

_____

**HIKE TYPE**  ↻ loop   ⇄ out and back   → one way   ☀ day trip   ⛺ overnight   other _____

**DISTANCE** _____

**ELEVATION** (gain/loss) _____

| **DIFFICULTY** | 1 | 2 | 3 | 4 | 5 | 6 | 7 | 8 | 9 | 10 |
|---|---|---|---|---|---|---|---|---|---|---|

**TERRAIN NOTES** _____

_____

**FACILITIES/WATER** _____

**WILDLIFE OBSERVED** _____

_____

_____

**HIGHLIGHTS** _____

_____

_____

_____

**OVERALL RATING**

# HIKING LOG

LOG #

**DATE**

**START TIME**

**END TIME**

**LOCATION**

**OBSERVATIONS**

WEATHER _____

ROUTE/TRAIL NAMES _____

_____

_____

_____

_____

HIKE TYPE    loop    out and back    one way    day trip    overnight    other _____

DISTANCE _____

ELEVATION (gain/loss) _____

**DIFFICULTY**    1    2    3    4    5    6    7    8    9    10

TERRAIN NOTES _____

_____

FACILITIES/WATER _____

WILDLIFE OBSERVED _____

_____

_____

HIGHLIGHTS _____

_____

_____

_____

OVERALL RATING

# HIKING LOG

LOG #

**DATE**

**START TIME**

**END TIME**

**LOCATION**

**OBSERVATIONS**

WEATHER _____

ROUTE/TRAIL NAMES _____

_____

_____

_____

_____

HIKE TYPE   ⟳ loop   ⇄ out and back   → one way   ☀ day trip   ⛺ overnight   other _____

DISTANCE _____

ELEVATION (gain/loss) _____

## DIFFICULTY   1   2   3   4   5   6   7   8   9   10

TERRAIN NOTES _____

_____

FACILITIES/WATER _____

WILDLIFE OBSERVED _____

_____

_____

HIGHLIGHTS _____

_____

_____

_____

OVERALL RATING   👢 👢 👢 👢 👢

# HIKING LOG

LOG #

**DATE**

**START TIME**

**END TIME**

**LOCATION**

OBSERVATIONS _____

**WEATHER** _____

**ROUTE/TRAIL NAMES** _____

_____

_____

_____

_____

**HIKE TYPE**   ◯ loop   ⇄ out and back   → one way   ☀ day trip   ⛺ overnight   other _____

**DISTANCE** _____

**ELEVATION** (gain/loss) _____

| DIFFICULTY | 1 | 2 | 3 | 4 | 5 | 6 | 7 | 8 | 9 | 10 |
|---|---|---|---|---|---|---|---|---|---|---|

**TERRAIN NOTES** _____

_____

**FACILITIES/WATER** _____

**WILDLIFE OBSERVED** _____

_____

_____

**HIGHLIGHTS** _____

_____

_____

_____

**OVERALL RATING** 🥾 🥾 🥾 🥾 🥾

# HIKING LOG

LOG #

**DATE**

**START TIME**

**END TIME**

**LOCATION**

**OBSERVATIONS**

WEATHER _____

ROUTE/TRAIL NAMES _____
_____
_____
_____
_____

HIKE TYPE   loop   out and back   one way   day trip   overnight   other _____

DISTANCE _____

ELEVATION (gain/loss) _____

## DIFFICULTY   1   2   3   4   5   6   7   8   9   10

TERRAIN NOTES _____
_____

FACILITIES/WATER _____

WILDLIFE OBSERVED _____
_____
_____

HIGHLIGHTS _____
_____
_____
_____

OVERALL RATING

# HIKING LOG

LOG #

DATE

START TIME

END TIME

LOCATION

OBSERVATIONS

**WEATHER** _____

**ROUTE/TRAIL NAMES** _____

_____

_____

_____

_____

**HIKE TYPE**   loop   out and back   one way   day trip   overnight   other _____

**DISTANCE** _____

**ELEVATION** (gain/loss) _____

| DIFFICULTY | 1 | 2 | 3 | 4 | 5 | 6 | 7 | 8 | 9 | 10 |
|---|---|---|---|---|---|---|---|---|---|---|

**TERRAIN NOTES** _____

_____

**FACILITIES/WATER** _____

**WILDLIFE OBSERVED** _____

_____

**HIGHLIGHTS** _____

_____

_____

_____

OVERALL RATING

# HIKING LOG

LOG #

**DATE**

**START TIME**

**END TIME**

**LOCATION**

**OBSERVATIONS**

WEATHER _____

ROUTE/TRAIL NAMES _____

_____

_____

_____

_____

HIKE TYPE    loop    out and back    one way    day trip    overnight    other _____

DISTANCE _____

ELEVATION (gain/loss) _____

| DIFFICULTY | 1 | 2 | 3 | 4 | 5 | 6 | 7 | 8 | 9 | 10 |
|---|---|---|---|---|---|---|---|---|---|---|

TERRAIN NOTES _____

_____

FACILITIES/WATER _____

WILDLIFE OBSERVED _____

_____

_____

HIGHLIGHTS _____

_____

_____

_____

OVERALL RATING

# HIKING LOG

LOG #

DATE

START TIME

END TIME

LOCATION

OBSERVATIONS

**WEATHER** _____

**ROUTE/TRAIL NAMES** _____

_____

_____

_____

_____

**HIKE TYPE**   ↻ loop   ⇄ out and back   → one way   ☀ day trip   ⛺ overnight   other _____

**DISTANCE** _____

**ELEVATION** (gain/loss) _____

| **DIFFICULTY** | 1 | 2 | 3 | 4 | 5 | 6 | 7 | 8 | 9 | 10 |

**TERRAIN NOTES** _____

_____

**FACILITIES/WATER** _____

**WILDLIFE OBSERVED** _____

_____

**HIGHLIGHTS** _____

_____

_____

_____

**OVERALL RATING**   🥾 🥾 🥾 🥾 🥾

# HIKING LOG

LOG #

**DATE**

**START TIME**

**END TIME**

**LOCATION**

**OBSERVATIONS**

WEATHER _____

ROUTE/TRAIL NAMES _____

_____

_____

_____

_____

HIKE TYPE   ↻        ⇄          →         ☀        ⛺        other _____
          loop   out and back  one way   day trip  overnight

DISTANCE _____

ELEVATION (gain/loss) _____

DIFFICULTY     1    2    3    4    5    6    7    8    9    10

TERRAIN NOTES _____

_____

FACILITIES/WATER _____

WILDLIFE OBSERVED _____

_____

_____

HIGHLIGHTS _____

_____

_____

_____

OVERALL RATING

# HIKING LOG

LOG #

**DATE**

**START TIME**

**END TIME**

**LOCATION**

**OBSERVATIONS**

**WEATHER** _____

**ROUTE/TRAIL NAMES** _____

_____

_____

_____

_____

**HIKE TYPE**   ⟳ loop   ⇄ out and back   → one way   ☀ day trip   ⛺ overnight   other _____

**DISTANCE** _____

**ELEVATION** (gain/loss) _____

**DIFFICULTY**   1   2   3   4   5   6   7   8   9   10

**TERRAIN NOTES** _____

_____

**FACILITIES/WATER** _____

**WILDLIFE OBSERVED** _____

_____

_____

**HIGHLIGHTS** _____

_____

_____

_____

**OVERALL RATING**

# HIKING LOG

LOG #

**DATE**

**START TIME**

**END TIME**

**LOCATION**

**OBSERVATIONS**

WEATHER _____

ROUTE/TRAIL NAMES _____

_____

_____

_____

_____

HIKE TYPE ◯ loop ⇄ out and back → one way ☀ day trip ⛺ overnight other _____

DISTANCE _____

ELEVATION (gain/loss) _____

**DIFFICULTY**   1   2   3   4   5   6   7   8   9   10

TERRAIN NOTES _____

_____

FACILITIES/WATER _____

WILDLIFE OBSERVED _____

_____

_____

HIGHLIGHTS _____

_____

_____

_____

OVERALL RATING 👢 👢 👢 👢 👢

# HIKING LOG

**LOG #**

**DATE**

**START TIME**

**END TIME**

**LOCATION**

**OBSERVATIONS**

**WEATHER** _____

**ROUTE/TRAIL NAMES** _____

_____

_____

_____

_____

**HIKE TYPE**     loop     out and back     one way     day trip     overnight     other _____

**DISTANCE** _____

**ELEVATION** (gain/loss) _____

| DIFFICULTY | 1 | 2 | 3 | 4 | 5 | 6 | 7 | 8 | 9 | 10 |
|---|---|---|---|---|---|---|---|---|---|---|

**TERRAIN NOTES** _____

_____

**FACILITIES/WATER** _____

**WILDLIFE OBSERVED** _____

_____

_____

**HIGHLIGHTS** _____

_____

_____

_____

**OVERALL RATING**

# HIKING LOG

LOG #

DATE

START TIME

END TIME

LOCATION

OBSERVATIONS

WEATHER _____

ROUTE/TRAIL NAMES _____

_____

_____

_____

_____

HIKE TYPE  ⟳ loop   ⇄ out and back   → one way   ☀ day trip   ⛺ overnight   other _____

DISTANCE _____

ELEVATION (gain/loss) _____

| DIFFICULTY | 1 | 2 | 3 | 4 | 5 | 6 | 7 | 8 | 9 | 10 |
|---|---|---|---|---|---|---|---|---|---|---|

TERRAIN NOTES _____

_____

FACILITIES/WATER _____

WILDLIFE OBSERVED _____

_____

_____

HIGHLIGHTS _____

_____

_____

_____

OVERALL RATING  👢 👢 👢 👢 👢

"METHINKS THAT THE MOMENT MY LEGS BEGIN TO MOVE,
MY THOUGHTS BEGIN TO FLOW."

—Henry David Thoreau

"YOU NEVER CLIMB THE SAME MOUNTAIN TWICE, NOT EVEN IN MEMORY.
MEMORY REBUILDS THE MOUNTAIN, CHANGES THE WEATHER,
RETELLS THE JOKES, REMAKES ALL THE MOVES."

—Lito Tejada-Flores

"THOSE WHO DWELL AMONG THE BEAUTIES AND MYSTERIES OF THE EARTH ARE NEVER ALONE OR WEARY OF LIFE."

—Rachel Carson

"THERE ARE NO SHORTCUTS TO ANY PLACE WORTH GOING."

—Beverly Sills

"I WAS AMAZED THAT WHAT I NEEDED TO SURVIVE COULD
BE CARRIED ON MY BACK. AND, MOST SURPRISING
OF ALL, THAT I COULD CARRY IT."

—Cheryl Strayed

"IT IS NOT THE MOUNTAIN WE CONQUER, BUT OURSELVES."

—Sir Edmund Hillary

"HAPPINESS AND HIKING GO HAND IN HAND OR FOOT IN BOOT."

—Diane Spicer

"WILDERNESS IS NOT A LUXURY BUT A NECESSITY OF
THE HUMAN SPIRIT, AND AS VITAL TO OUR LIVES
AS WATER AND GOOD BREAD."

—Edward Abbey

"NOW I SEE THE SECRET OF MAKING THE BEST PERSON:
IT IS TO GROW IN THE OPEN AIR AND TO EAT AND
SLEEP WITH THE EARTH."
—Walt Whitman

HIKING CHECKLISTS

# MY ALL-TIME FAVORITE HIKING TRIPS

**KEEP YOUR GREATEST HIKING MOMENTS** fresh in your mind, and never forget the mountaintops you'd like to return to someday. List your truly unforgettable hiking trips here.

| DATE | LOCATION |
|------|----------|

HIGHLIGHTS

| DATE | LOCATION |
|------|----------|

HIGHLIGHTS

**DATE**

**LOCATION**

HIGHLIGHTS _____

_____

_____

_____

_____

_____

_____


**DATE**

**LOCATION**

HIGHLIGHTS _____

_____

_____

_____

_____

_____

_____


**DATE**

**LOCATION**

HIGHLIGHTS _____

_____

_____

_____

_____

_____

# MY HIKING BUCKET LIST

**HERE'S WHERE YOU CAN DREAM BIG:** List the famous trails you'd like to explore, mountains you yearn to climb, or far-flung campsites where you'd love to spend the night. Once you achieve one of the goals on this list, check it off with pride.

# MY ESSENTIAL GEAR

FOR SAFE AND ENJOYABLE HIKING, it's essential to load up your pack with some key equipment. Create a personalized checklist of your go-to gear here.

- [ ] _____
- [ ] _____
- [ ] _____
- [ ] _____
- [ ] _____
- [ ] _____
- [ ] _____
- [ ] _____
- [ ] _____
- [ ] _____
- [ ] _____
- [ ] _____
- [ ] _____
- [ ] _____
- [ ] _____
- [ ] _____
- [ ] _____
- [ ] _____

# MOUNTAINS I'VE CLIMBED

KEEP A RUNNING LIST OF EVERY MOUNTAIN you've scaled,
from your local glorified hill to the snowiest Alpine peaks.

| MOUNTAIN NAME | DATE CLIMBED |
|---|---|
| MOUNTAIN NAME | DATE CLIMBED |
| MOUNTAIN NAME | DATE CLIMBED |
| MOUNTAIN NAME | DATE CLIMBED |
| MOUNTAIN NAME | DATE CLIMBED |
| MOUNTAIN NAME | DATE CLIMBED |
| MOUNTAIN NAME | DATE CLIMBED |
| MOUNTAIN NAME | DATE CLIMBED |
| MOUNTAIN NAME | DATE CLIMBED |

# MOUNTAINS I'VE CLIMBED

| MOUNTAIN NAME | DATE CLIMBED |
|---|---|
| MOUNTAIN NAME | DATE CLIMBED |
| MOUNTAIN NAME | DATE CLIMBED |
| MOUNTAIN NAME | DATE CLIMBED |
| MOUNTAIN NAME | DATE CLIMBED |
| MOUNTAIN NAME | DATE CLIMBED |
| MOUNTAIN NAME | DATE CLIMBED |
| MOUNTAIN NAME | DATE CLIMBED |
| MOUNTAIN NAME | DATE CLIMBED |
| MOUNTAIN NAME | DATE CLIMBED |
| MOUNTAIN NAME | DATE CLIMBED |

# WILDLIFE I'VE ENCOUNTERED

ON THESE PAGES, RECORD all the animal species you've spotted from the trail, whether it's a common squirrel or an elusive mountain lion.

| ANIMAL | DATE SEEN | LOCATION |
|--------|-----------|----------|
|  |  |  |
|  |  |  |
|  |  |  |
|  |  |  |
|  |  |  |
|  |  |  |
|  |  |  |
|  |  |  |
|  |  |  |
|  |  |  |
|  |  |  |
|  |  |  |
|  |  |  |

# WILDLIFE I'VE ENCOUNTERED

| ANIMAL | DATE SEEN | LOCATION |
|--------|-----------|----------|
|        |           |          |
|        |           |          |
|        |           |          |
|        |           |          |
|        |           |          |
|        |           |          |
|        |           |          |
|        |           |          |
|        |           |          |
|        |           |          |
|        |           |          |
|        |           |          |
|        |           |          |
|        |           |          |
|        |           |          |
|        |           |          |
|        |           |          |
|        |           |          |

# THE
# HIKER'S JOURNAL

## weldon**owen**

www.weldonowen.com

ISBN: 978-1-68188-644-2

PRINTED IN CHINA

10 9 8 7 6 5 4

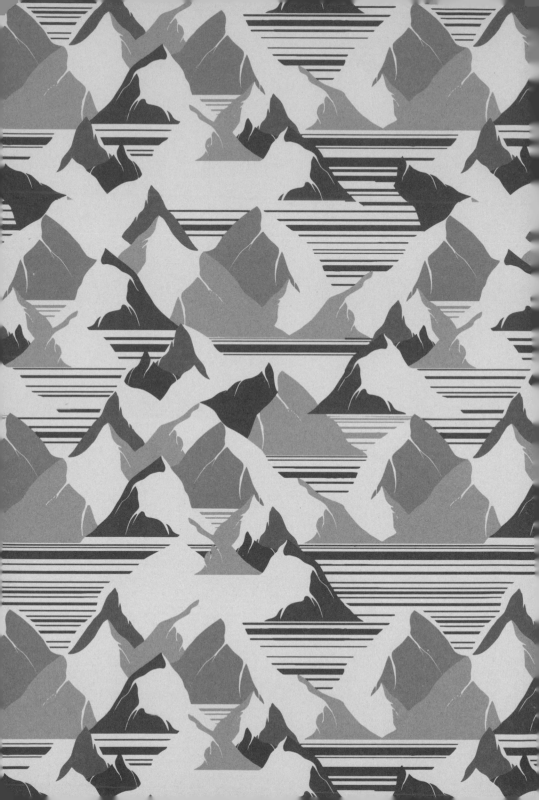